There Is No White Bear In The Room

By: MCGrace Johnsen

Illustrated by: Andres V. Garcia

Dear Parents & Teachers:

We hope that this book can help your children become more open minded with the unknown.

Sooner or later our worries will catch up to us; we must learn to face them.

"Sometimes it may seem easier to ignore things that bother you. It may appear to pass, but chances are it will never completely disappear. Sooner or later your worries will catch up to you; we must learn to face the unknown."

~MCGrace Johnsen

AUTHOR

Mary Cynthia Grace M. Johnsen, also known as Grace, has her Master's Degree in Mental Health Counseling and is a National Certified Counselor. Her specialty is working with children. Besides two little girls of her own, she loved working with the children at Center for Child and Family Services, Hampton, Virginia and Armed Forces YMCA, Virginia Beach, Virginia in their Elementary Schools' Anti-Bullying Program. She often used cognitive behavioral therapy and play therapy well. She has written books with applied psychotherapy to teach handling techniques on hard to manage emotions such as anxiety and anger. Her last book entitled, <u>Don't Be Afraid</u>, can be found on Amazon.com and BarnesAndNoble.com.

Grace met her next illustrator, Andres Garcia, while working as behavior therapists for children in the Autism Spectrum House, in Navarre, Florida.

ILLUSTRATOR

Andres Vicente Garcia has loved art since he was a toddler. The fact that he could think of an idea and make it come to life really motivated him to grow in his art skills. Andres graduated from Navarre High School where he was a member of the National Art Society. He then continued his education and graduated with a Bachelors in Psychology from Spring Hill College. He took several art courses at Spring Hill to continue his love for his hobby and as a way to clear his mind from his studies. Besides working as a child behavioral health counselor for children in the Autism Spectrum, Andres is now pursuing physical therapy school and continues to create and "play" with art in his free time. <u>There Is No White Bear in the Room</u> is his first published children's book that he has illustrated for. A lot of time and energy was spent dedicated to this hard work, by evidence of all the images drawn by hand.

Thank you to:

My dear husband, Timothy Johnsen, for being very supportive of my career.

My two very wonderful daughters, Hannah (age 5) and Isabelle (age 2), for being my inspiration.

My teachers, supervisors, and colleagues for being my motivation into making my dreams come true.

Special thanks to:

Andres V. Garcia for being my illustrator for this book. You are very talented and without you, I could not have made all this happen.

This book is dedicated to:

HANNAH

There is no white bear in the room.

There is no red cake in the room.

There is no blue elephant in the room.

There is no yellow monkey in the room.

Some of these things may seem a bit weird,

but what would you do if they suddenly appeared?

What if you try to meet the white bear?

What if...

...you try to taste the red cake?

What if ...

...you try to hear the blue elephant?

Would you be excited for the odd things inside?

Or would you rather go somewhere else and just hide?

The white bear may be big and loud when he ROARS.

But he may want to play games
and help with your chores.

The red cake
may look
YUCKY
and taste like
feet.

Or it could
taste sweeter
than your
favorite treat.

The blue elephant may be too loud.

What can you do?

You can put on headphones and
ride with him too!

The yellow monkey is neat but, how does he smell?

He could smell *fresh*, as far as you can tell.

But what if he smells just a bit *foul*.

Can we give him a bath and a fresh new towel?

You may think it is easy to avoid what you fear.
It may seem to go away but it won't disappear.
The bear may look big, he may want to play.
And that cake may be great, or simply okay.
That blue elephant may be quiet, or shout.
But you never will know unless you figure it out.

So be happy
to find something
that you don't know.

Ask a friend
or a parent for some help
and just go.

I think you will find
there is no trouble you see.

Something you were afraid of
may be fun, actually.